100%
MINE

CONSENT (FOR KIDS!)

BOUNDARIES, RESPECT, AND BEING IN CHARGE of YOU

RACHEL BRIAN

LITTLE, BROWN AND COMPANY
NEW YORK BOSTON

TO MY THREE CHILDREN, LOLA, MILO & ENZO,
WHO INSPIRE ME WITH THEIR FIERCE UNIQUENESS,
BRING SO MUCH LOVE INTO MY LIFE,
AND OCCASIONALLY EVEN MAKE THEIR OWN CHEESE PLATES.

ABOUT THIS BOOK

The illustrations for this book were rendered digitally. This book was edited by Lisa Yoskowitz and designed by Karina Granda. The production was supervised by Erika Schwartz, and the production editor was Annie McDonnell. The text was set in ConsentForKids, and the display type is hand-lettered.

Little, Brown and Company | Hachette Book Group | 1290 Avenue of the Americas, New York, NY 10104
Visit us at LBYR.com | First Edition: January 2020 | Little, Brown and Company is a division of Hachette Book Group, Inc. The Little, Brown name and logo are trademarks of Hachette Book Group, Inc.

The publisher is not responsible for websites (or their content) that are not owned by the publisher.

Library of Congress Control Number: 2019946166

ISBNs: 978-0-316-45773-6 (hardcover), 978-0-316-45777-4 (ebook), 978-0-316-45778-1 (ebook), 978-0-316-45779-8 (ebook) I Printed in China I APS I 10 9 8 7 6 5 4 3 2

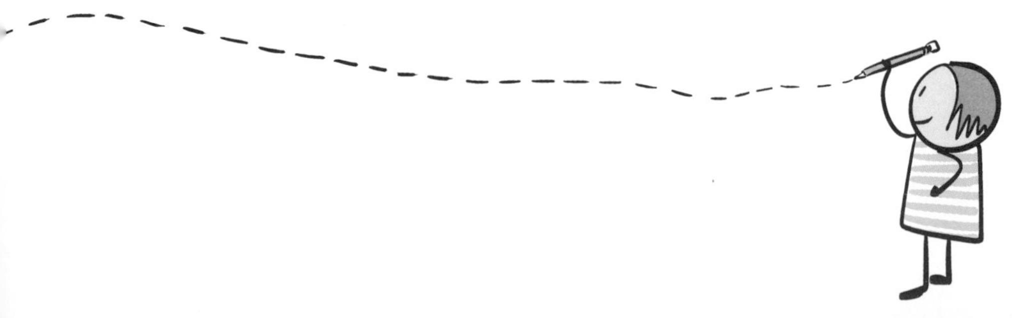

WELCOME!

THIS BOOK IS FOR YOU.

YAY! I LOVE STUFF FOR ME!
for: YOU!

BTW — THESE ARE ALL YOU.

OK, NONE OF THEM LOOK **EXACTLY** LIKE YOU. (I HEARD YOU HAVE A NOSE.) BUT LET'S SAY THEY'RE YOU...

WHAT THIS BOOK **CAN** DO:

HELP YOU UNDERSTAND & PRACTICE CONSENT
YES, INDEED!
HELP YOU BUILD STRONG FRIENDSHIPS
SUGGEST WAYS TO GET HELP

WHAT IT **CAN'T** DO:

SING YOU A SILLY SONG
Socks are great!

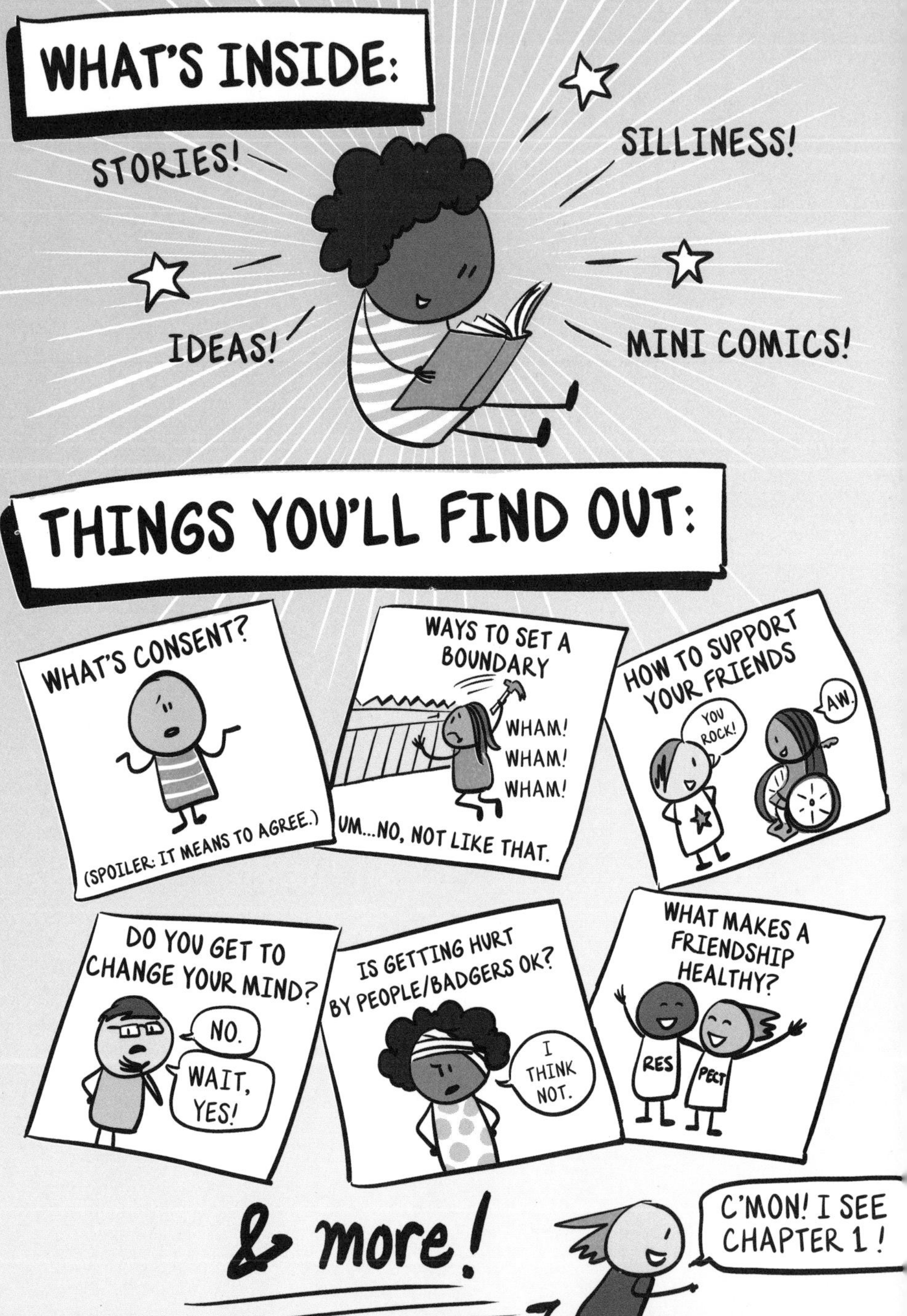
WHAT'S INSIDE:
STORIES!
SILLINESS!
IDEAS!
MINI COMICS!
THINGS YOU'LL FIND OUT:
WHAT'S CONSENT?
(SPOILER: IT MEANS TO AGREE.)
WAYS TO SET A BOUNDARY
WHAM! WHAM! WHAM!
UM...NO, NOT LIKE THAT.
HOW TO SUPPORT YOUR FRIENDS
YOU ROCK!
AW.
DO YOU GET TO CHANGE YOUR MIND?
NO.
WAIT, YES!
IS GETTING HURT BY PEOPLE/BADGERS OK?
I THINK NOT.
WHAT MAKES A FRIENDSHIP HEALTHY?
RES
PECT
& more!
C'MON! I SEE CHAPTER 1!

chapter 1 YOU RULE

AW, THANKS!

CONSENT

T'S LIKE BEING THE RULER OF YOUR OWN COUNTRY.
POPULATION: **YOU**.

I hearby decree that I won't be doing any snuggling today.

BEING THE RULER OF YOUR BODY MEANS:

100% MINE.
in control of own body

YOUR BODY IS YOURS.

AS A RULER...
YOU GET TO SET YOUR OWN
BOUNDARIES.

AWESOME!

UMM...WAIT, WHAT'S A BOUNDARY?

A BOUNDARY IS A LIMIT.

YOUR BOUNDARIES ARE LIKE A LINE BETWEEN WHAT YOU'RE COMFORTABLE WITH. . .

LET'S SWAP HATS!
OK!

WANNA SHARE MY FRIES?
YES!

LET'S GO TO MY HOUSE!
YEAH!

C'MON! LET'S JUMP!
YAY!

AND WHAT YOU ARE NOT COMFORTABLE WITH...

LET'S TRADE UNDERWEAR!
Ew, no.
WANT THIS FRY? I ONLY CHEWED IT A LITTLE.
NO THANKS!
LET'S GO TO MY NEIGHBOR'S HOUSE!
UMM NO. LET'S GO TO YOUR HOUSE.
C'MON, LET'S JUMP!
LET'S NOT.

YOU MAY HAVE DIFFERENT BOUNDARIES for DIFFERENT PEOPLE

AND TIMES WHEN BOUNDARIES **CHANGE.**

THERE ARE LOTS OF WAYS TO BE SOCIAL:

HIGH-FIVING!
HUGGING!
NODDING!
NO TOUCHING, PLEASE.
WAVING!
I ONLY HUG SNOOKUMS...
SNOOKUMS
KITTY SNUGGLING.

HMMM...
WHAT BOUNDARIES SHOULD I HAVE?

IT'S UP TO YOU.
OOOH... NICE!

BODILY AUTONOMY means

I LIKE IT!
BUT CAN I
PRONOUNCE IT?

HAVING A CHOICE ABOUT WHAT YOU DO WITH YOUR BODY.

SO WHEN AUNT GLADYS SAYS:

COME HERE!
I WANT TO PINCH
& KISS THOSE
CHEEKS!

GUESS WHAT?

YOU STILL DECIDE.

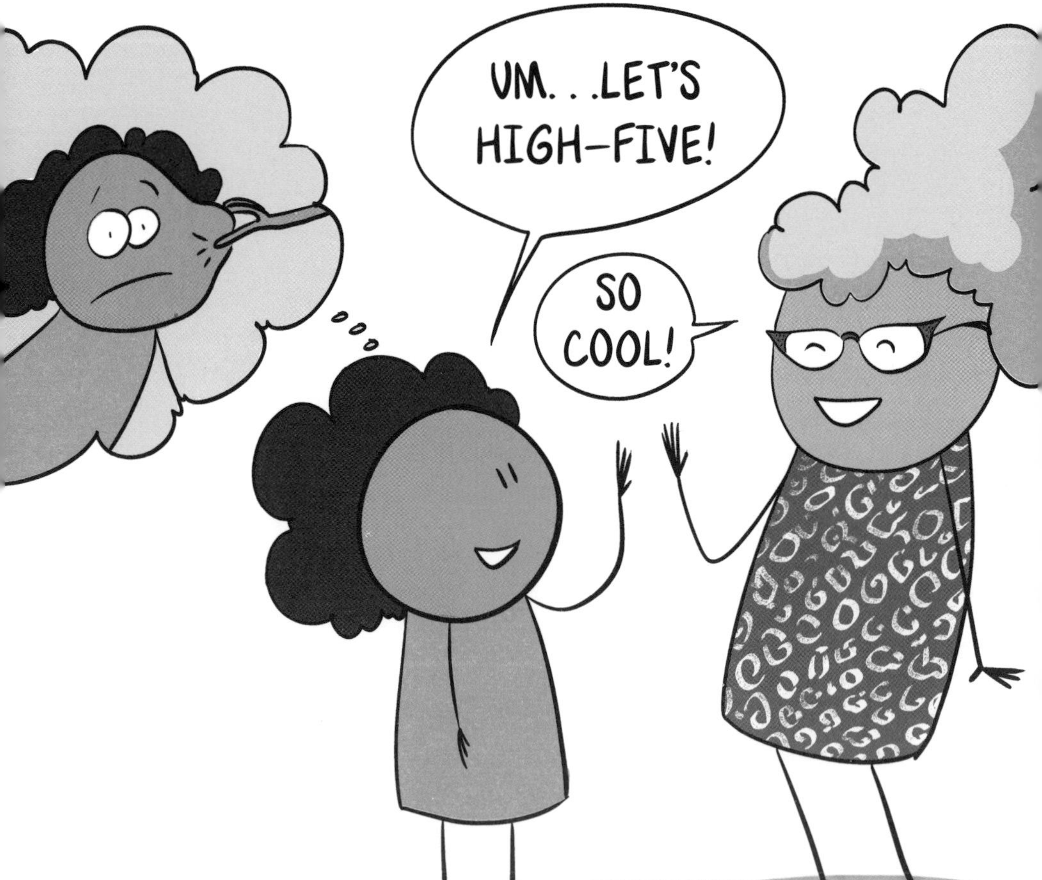
UM. . .LET'S HIGH-FIVE!
SO COOL!

OK, SURE...

THERE ARE TIMES WHEN WE DO STUFF TO KEEP OURSELVES OR OTHERS SAFE & WE DON'T GET TO DECIDE.

LIKE HOLDING HANDS IN A BUSY PARKING LOT.

OR TAKING MEDICINE SO WE GET WELL.

!
SORRY, THIS ONE'S NOT OPTIONAL.
TRUSTED ADULT

DON'T WALK

OR WAITING FOR THE LIGHT SO WE CAN CROSS THE STREET.

BUT YOU STILL GET TO HAVE A SAY...

THAT'S TOO TIGHT— IT HURTS.
OOPS, SORRY.
SURE! NO PROBLEM.
I'M SCARED. I NEED TO TAKE A FEW DEEP BREATHS FIRST.
AT LEAST I CAN CHOOSE HOW I WAIT.
YAWN
DON'T WALK

chapter 2 TRUST YOUR GUT!

I'M TRYNA TELL YOU SOMETHING!

YOUR GUT HELPS YOU FIGURE OUT WHAT YOU ARE COMFORTABLE WITH:

Might feel good!
Might not feel good!
SOLO ADVENTURE!
YAY!
eek!
ICE CREAM!
YUM!
ICE CREAM!
EW! GROSS.
HEY! WANT A RIDE?
MOM
YAY!
!
HEY! WANT A RIDE?
NEIGHBORHOOD BULLY
YIKES! ALERT!

IF YOUR GUT DECIDES THAT SOMEONE'S ATTENTION GIVES YO

A SLIGHTLY **ICKY** FEELING...

Awkward!

OR A **VERY** ICKY FEELING...

gulp!
GAMER82
HI!
HI?
SEND PICS
WHAT'S UR NAME?
WANNA MEET?

IT'S OK TO SAY NO TO THEIR ATTENTION.

IF A PERSON DOESN'T RESPECT YOUR BOUNDARY OR PRESSURES YOU TO CHANGE YOUR MIND, IT'S IMPORTANT TO TELL A:

NOT EVERYONE IS HELPFUL, THOUGH. PICK SOMEONE WHO IS KIND & HAS THE ABILITY TO HELP YOU.

chapter 3 GIVING & GETTING CONSENT

DO ASK,
DO TELL.

EVERYONE'S BOUNDARIES ARE DIFFERENT,

O IT'S IMPORTANT TO FIND OUT WHAT SOMEONE CONSENTS TO.

ARE YOU IN A HUGGY MOOD?
Nope.

TO CONSENT MEANS TO AGREE TO SOMETHING.

ESPECIALLY WHEN IT HAS TO DO WITH OUR BODIES.

LET'S SAY YOU HELP SOMEONE CROSS THE STREE

NICE, RIGHT?
I'LL HELP YOU!
UNLESS...
THEY DON'T WANT TO BE HELPED.
(THEN YOU'RE JUST GRABBING A STRANGER
Aaaah!
Whap!
Whap!
Whap!
WAIT! I'M HELPING

THE OTHER PERSON HAS TO CONSENT.

GOT IT.

AND WHAT ABOUT PINCHING?

NOT NICE, RIGHT?
RIGHT! I HATE GETTING PINCHED!
UNLESS...
OKAY.
PINCH ME! I THINK I'M DREAMING!
THANKS!
PINCH!
JJ Reyes
$5,000,000

THERE ARE **2** PARTS OF CONSENT.

1. PRACTICE TELLING PEOPLE HOW YOU FEEL:

I FEEL LIKE **DANCING!**
I FEEL TOO TIRED TO DO **ANYTHING!**

I WANT TO TRY THAT!
I DO NOT WANT TO TRY THAT.

HINT: BE **CLEAR & DIRECT.**

(IT GETS EASIER THE MORE YOU DO IT!)

2. PRACTICE **LISTENING** TO OTHERS.

TRY IT!
I DON'T WANT ANY!
OK! MMM... YUM!
gulp!

BECAUSE SOMETHING THAT'S NO BIG DEAL TO YOU...

MIGHT BE A REALLY BIG DEAL TO SOMEONE ELSE.

HOW DO YOU **KNOW** IF SOMEONE CONSENTS?

IS THERE SOME **MAGIC** WAY TO TELL?

GOOD NEWS! There is.

ASK THEM!

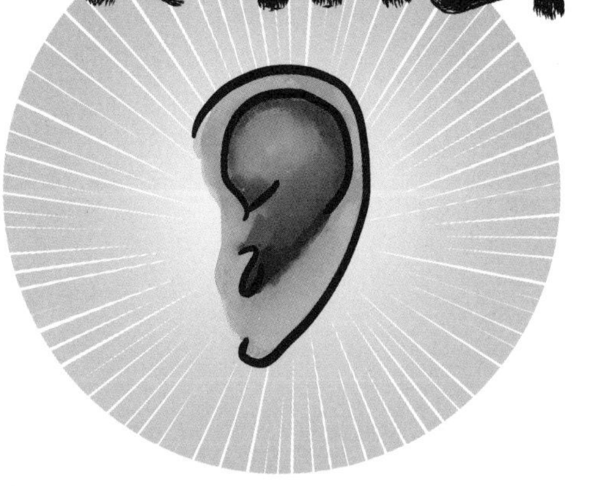

(AND LISTEN TO THE ANSWER.)

SOMETIMES THE ANSWER IS VERY CLEAR

& OTHER TIMES IT'S **NOT** SO DIRECT.

SAYS "YES" BUT LOOKS SCARED

FREEZES UP

SHRUGS

CHANGES THE SUBJECT

ARE THESE CLEARLY **CONSENT**?

WHEN A PERSON USES POWER TO GET SOMEONE TO AGREE...

GIVE ME THAT CHEESE!
OK! DON'T HURT ME!

THAT'S STILL

NOT

CONSENT.

DOES SOMEONE'S OUTFIT TELL YOU IF THEY CONSENT?

NO.

LET'S PUSH THEM IN!
YEAH, THEY'VE GOT A BATHING SUIT ON!
ABSOLUTELY NOT!
NO CONSENT

DON'T ASSUME YOU KNOW WHY SOMEONE IS DRESSED IN A PARTICULAR WAY.

YOU MUST BE EXCITED TO SWIM!
NO, ACTUALLY, I JUST LIKE WEARING THIS. I'M PLANNING TO WEAR IT TO DINNER!

PEOPLE HAVE THEIR OWN REASONS FOR DRESSING THE WAY THEY DO.

brrr...

FEELS COLD

DOESN'T WANT TO BE RECOGNIZED

IS HIDING THEIR DOG IN THERE

CLOTHING ISN'T CONSENT.

YEAH. OBVIOUSLY!

SO LISTEN AND LOOK FOR

CLEAR CONSENT,

ESPECIALLY WHEN IT INVOLVES SOMEONE'S **BODY.**

IF YOU'RE NOT SURE—

IT'S A **NO.**

NEWS FLASH!

PEOPLE MIGHT CROSS YOUR BOUNDARIES WITHOUT MEANING TO...

HUGS!
eep!
NO HUGS

NO HUGS.
OHHH. OK.

MAKE SURE TO TELL THEM SO THEY CAN LEARN WHAT YOUR BOUNDARIES ARE.

THE TICKLING

A MINI COMIC

I'M BORED.
YEAH.
I THOUGHT OF SOMETHING FUN!
YA?
I'LL TICKLE YOU!
PASS.
C'MON! YOU'RE SOO TICKLISH!
HEY! CUT IT OUT! HA HA HA STOP!
HA HA HA NO HA HAHAHA HA HA
SEE! IT'S FUN!!
HAHAHA HA HA HA HAHA HAHAHA HAhA HA HA HA HA GASP
FUN. RIGHT?
UM... NOT FUN?
GET OUT!
THE END.

THE TICKLING TAKE 2

IN A PARALLEL UNIVERSE...

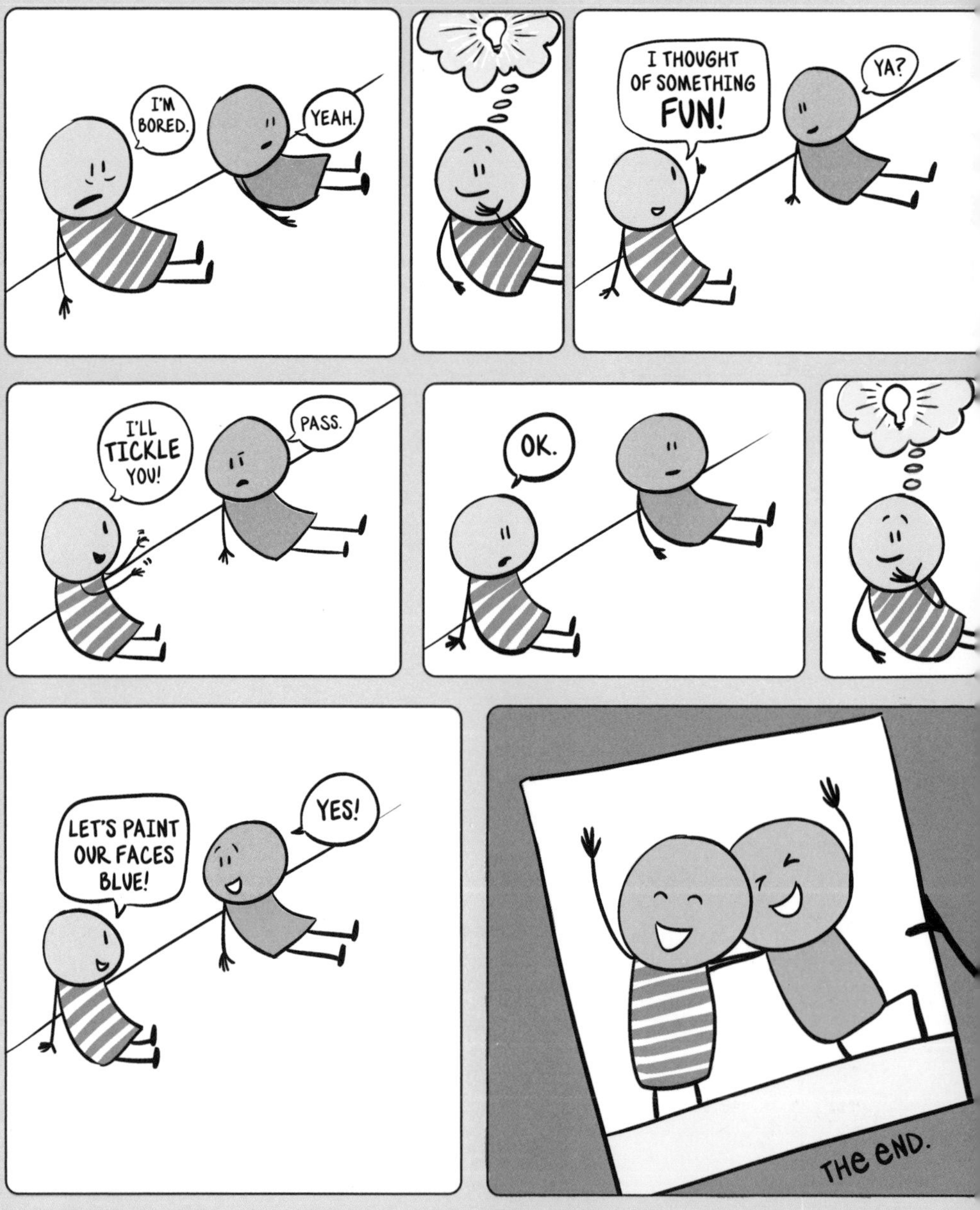
I'M BORED.
YEAH.
I THOUGHT OF SOMETHING FUN!
YA?
I'LL TICKLE YOU!
PASS.
OK.
LET'S PAINT OUR FACES BLUE!
YES!
THE END.

chapter 4 THANKS, but NO THANKS

IT'S OK TO CHANGE YOUR MIND!

O YOU SET A
OUNDARY THAT
OESN'T FEEL RIGHT...

FEAR NOT!

CHANGING YOUR MIND
IS A-OK!

UH-OH!
SNAKES OK
?
AAAAAH! COBRA!!
SNAKES OK
ACTUALLY... THAT LOOKS KINDA TASTY.
BSOLUTELY
O COCONUT
OUGHNUTS.
mmm... COCONUT!
ABSOLUTELY NO COCONUT DOUGHNUTS.

IMAGINE YOU MEET AN ADORABLE ALIEN.

HI! I'M GLURG

GLURG WANTS A HUG TO CELEBRATE INTERGALACTIC PEACE & FRIENDSHIP:

HUG?
SURE!

BUT IT'S NOT QUITE WHAT YOU THOUGHT:

EEK!
MUAHAHA!!!

IT'S OK TO CHANGE YOUR MIND

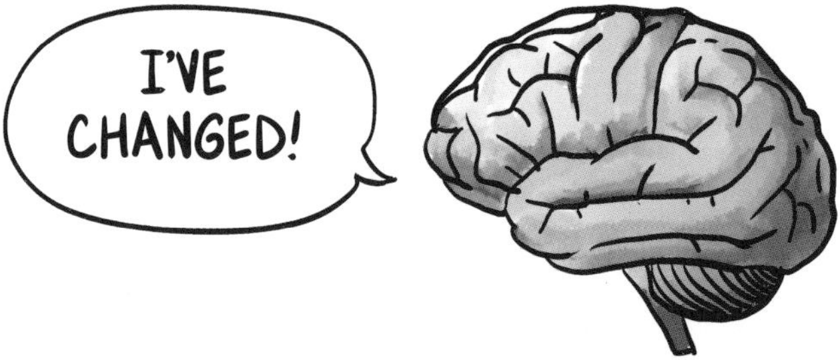
I'VE CHANGED!

YOU DID WANT TO HUG.

ACTUALLY, LET'S JUST WAVE.
DARN. OK.

NOW YOU DON'T.

WHEW.

IT'S THAT SIMPLE.

OR MAYBE YOU **TRIED** SOMETHING, BUT YOU DIDN'T LIKE IT AFTER ALL.

THROWING PIES IN MY FACE? **YUM!** LET'S DO IT!
CONSENT

OW!

IT'S **STILL** OK TO CHANGE YOUR MIND.

(Even if you've said "yes" a million times before!)

HERE COMES ANOTHER ONE!
NO! NO MORE PIES!
OH, OK.
NO MORE CONSENT.

NEWS FLASH!

SOMETIMES PEOPLE GET UPSET IF YOU CHANGE YOUR MIND.

BUT YOU SAID YOU WOULD!
YOU WANTED TO YESTERDAY.
BUT YOU PROMISED!
YOU ARE A LIAR!

THEY MIGHT GET FRUSTRATED, ANNOYED, OR EVEN ANGRY.

BUT YOU STILL GET TO DECIDE.

STILL MY BODY!

THE BADGER

A MINI COMIC ABOUT RELATIONSHIP BOUNDARIES

I BROUGHT YOU THIS BADGER!
UM...THANKS?
I GUESS YOU'RE KINDA CUTE.
WOW! YOUR OWN BADGER! COOL!
I KNOW, RIGHT?
THIS IS GREAT!
THIS BADGER IS SO SWEET!
AAAH! I MEAN USUALLY...
AW, SEE?! YOU REALLY ARE NICE!
EEK!
AW...IT'S OK, HOW CAN I STAY MAD AT YOU?
POW!
CHOMP!
BAP!
THIS ISN'T WORKING OUT. I NEED A NEW BOUNDARY.
WILDLIFE REHAB
NO BADGERS
THE END

THE BADGER 2: THE SEQUE

THE NEXT TIME:

I BROUGHT YOU THIS BADGER!
!
MY LAST BADGER DIDN'T REALLY WORK OUT...
EVEN THOUGH IT WAS CUTE, AND EVERYONE THOUGHT IT WAS COOL—IT WAS REALLY DANGEROUS & ATTACKED ME.
THAT'S WHY I GOT THIS SIGN!
NO BADGERS.
NOW I'M LOOKING FOR A PET THAT'S SAFE, LEGAL, & LIKES TO SNUGGLE.
OOH! PICK ME!
THE END

chapter 5 GROW HEALTHY RELATIONSHIPS

THERE ARE MANY KINDS OF RELATIONSHIPS:

PARENT

SIBLING

PET

EXTENDED FAMILY

FRIEND

TEACHER OR COACH

PROFESSIONAL

ROMANTIC

STRANGER

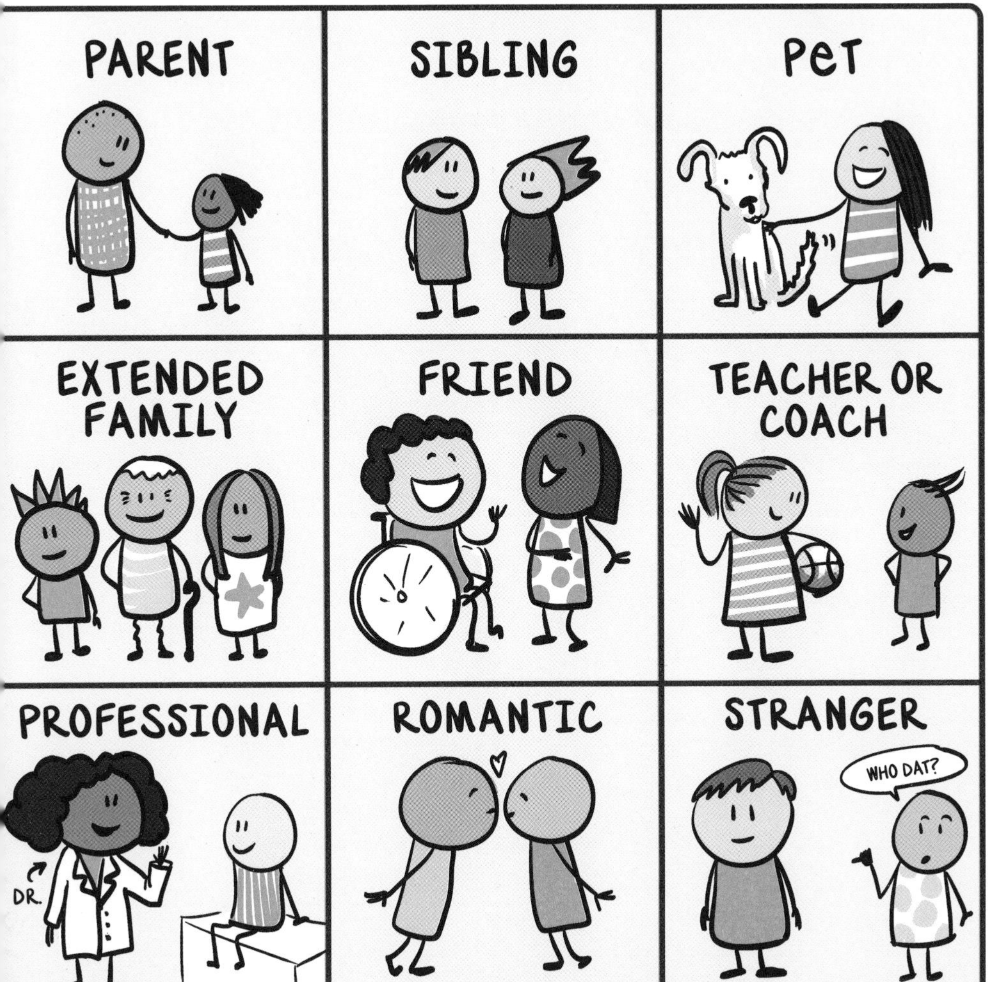

HOW DO YOU KNOW IF A RELATIONSHIP IS HEALTHY?

ONE WAY TO FIND OUT IS TO ASK:
HOW DOES BEING AROUND THIS PERSON MAKE ME FEEL?
SAFE & RESPECTED—YOU CAN BE YOURSELF!
YOU LIKE ME EVEN WHEN I WEAR MY SILLY OVERALLS.
YES!
WORRIED ABOUT MAKING THE OTHER PERSON ANGRY.
OH NO! IF I'M LATE THEY'LL YELL AT ME!
BEWARE!
BAD ABOUT YOURSELF.
I'M STUPID, UGLY & THE WORST.
UH-OH.
HAPPY AND EXCITED ABOUT THE FUTURE.
LET'S GO HAVE FUN!
WOO-HOO!

THERE ARE DIFFICULT MOMENTS IN ALL RELATIONSHIPS.

UT YOU CAN WORK HROUGH THEM BY **TALKING** ABOUT & **RESPECTING** ACH OTHER'S OUNDARIES.

I FEEL SAD WHEN YOU MAKE FUN OF ME.
OH, OK! I'LL TRY NOT TO DO THAT ANYMORE.

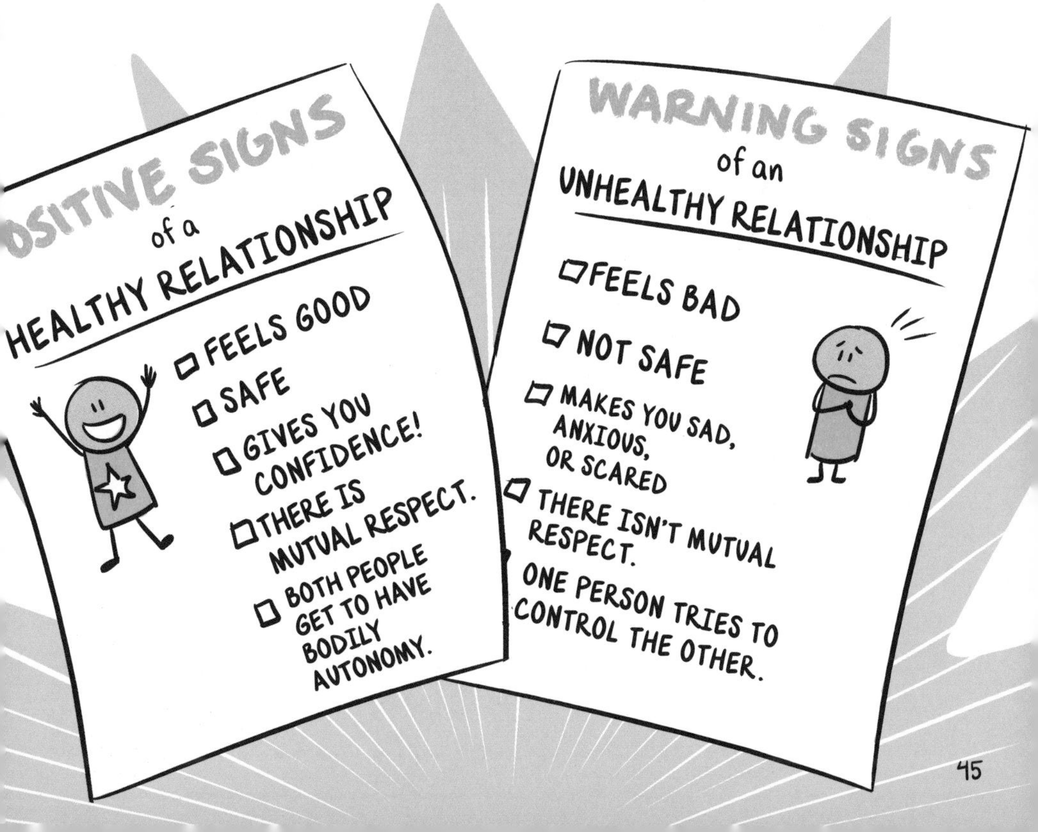

OSITIVE SIGNS of a HEALTHY RELATIONSHIP
FEELS GOOD
SAFE
GIVES YOU CONFIDENCE!
THERE IS MUTUAL RESPECT.
BOTH PEOPLE GET TO HAVE BODILY AUTONOMY.
WARNING SIGNS of an UNHEALTHY RELATIONSHIP
FEELS BAD
NOT SAFE
MAKES YOU SAD, ANXIOUS, OR SCARED
THERE ISN'T MUTUAL RESPECT.
ONE PERSON TRIES TO CONTROL THE OTHER.

NEWS FLASH!
IF SOMEONE BRIBES YOU
OR THREATENS YOU TO GET YOU TO DO SOMETHING,
THAT'S NOT CONSENT.

MOST PEOPLE WHO SEEM NICE ARE, WELL... **NICE!**

I'M LEGIT.

SO USUALLY WHEN A PERSON WORKS HARD TO GAIN YOUR TRUST,

GIFT GIVING
COMPLIMENTS
YOU'RE THE BEST!
ATTENTION
I CAN HELP YOU.
YAY!
BECOMING AN IMPORTANT PART OF YOUR LIFE
YOU'RE SPECIAL! I'M GONNA MAKE YOU A STAR.
WOO!

IT'S GREAT. YOU HAVE A PERSON TO MENTOR & SUPPORT YOU.

BUT SOME PEOPLE BUILD THAT TRUST T

BREAK IT.

THAT'S CALLED GROOMING.

WARNING SIGNS:

SECRECY
DON'T TELL.
?
ISOLATION
YAY! WE'RE ALONE!
INAPPROPRIATE TOUCHING OR REQUESTS
I HAVE AN IDEA...
!
THREATS AND CONTROL
DO IT OR ELSE.
?

THAT'S NOT YOUR FAULT.

WHEN AN ADULT IS INAPPROPRIATE WITH A KID, IT'S **ALWAYS** THE ADULT'S FAULT.

TRUST ISN'T SOMETHING YOU EARN AND THEN HAVE FOREVER.

IF SOMEONE YOU TRUST DOES SOMETHING THAT'S NOT OK, YOU CAN CHANGE YOUR MIND ABOUT THEM.

I'LL LOOK OUT FOR YOU.
YOU CAN TALK TO ME ANYTIME. I SUPPORT & BELIEVE YOU.
HERE 4 U
GOOD FRIEND
EARN EACH OTHER'S TRUS
EVERY DAY.

THEY ARE THERE FOR EACH OTHER.
HELP!
I'VE GOT YOUR BACK, FRIENDO!

chapter 6 REFLECT

WHO, ME?

WE CAN ALL REMEMBER A TIME* WHEN SOMEONE DIDN'T RESPECT OUR BOUNDARIES.

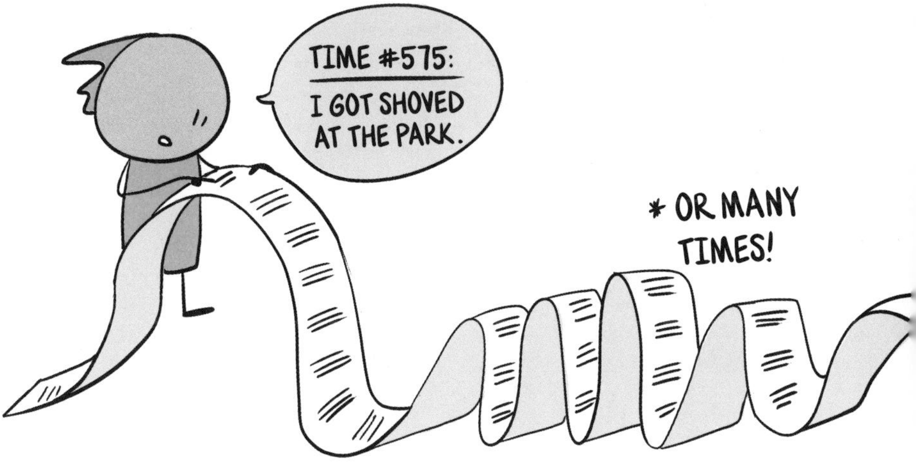

TIME #575:
I GOT SHOVED AT THE PARK.

* OR MANY TIMES!

BUT NOW IT'S TIME TO REFLECT!

HOW WELL DO **YOU** RESPECT OTHER PEOPLE'S BOUNDARIES?

ME A MINI COMIC

Hi!
I THINK I'M GREAT AT RESPECTING BOUNDARIES! HOLD ON A SEC...
HEY!
SHOVE!
LEMME JUST GET RID OF MY SIBLING. SO, I WAS SAYING...
YEAH, I'M REALLY GOOD AT...OH...HMMM...OK, WELL, NOT ALWAYS.
WAAAAH!
ESPECIALLY WHEN I WAS LITTLE. I'D HUG THE CAT EVEN THOUGH SHE DIDN'T LIKE IT...
Why me?
KITTY!
AND I'D DRAG MY BABY BROTHER AROUND...
C'MON!
NOOO!
AND I'D SHOVE MY FRIEND WHEN I WAS MAD.
Aaah!
BUT I'M TRYING TO GET BETTER AT IT...HMMM... RIGHT...
sniff
SORRY ABOUT THAT!

IT'S EASY TO FOCUS ON WHAT **YOU** WANT & FORGET TO LISTEN TO OTHERS.

C'MON.
NO...
PLEASE?
NO.
C'MON.
NO.
IF YOU DON'T, I WON'T BE YOUR FRIEND.
I DON'T WANT TO.
I'LL TELL YOUR SECRETS TO EVERYONE.
OK! I'LL DO IT.
ARE YOU TRYING TO **CONTROL** YOUR FRIENDS?
OR REALLY LISTENING FOR **CONSENT**?
NOPE NOPE NOPE NOPE!
C'MON!
I'M NOT SURE...
I'LL GIVE YOU MONEY.
I DON'T WANT TO.
C'MON, I'LL GIVE YOU A PRESENT.
OK, FINE, I GUESS...

SOMEONE'S BOUNDARIES EXIST EVEN WHEN THE PERSON ISN'T THERE WITH YOU...

WANNA HEAR SOMETHING CARL TOLD ME TO KEEP SECRET?!
UM...IF CARL WANTS ME TO KNOW—HE'LL TELL ME.
WANT ME TO SHARE THIS EMBARRASSING PICTURE OF MY FRIEND?
NO, THANKS, THAT'S FOR THEM TO DECIDE.

NEWS FLASH!

DON'T SHARE

PICTURES

OR

VIDEOS OF SOMEONE

WITHOUT THEIR CONSENT. (EVEN IF THEY SENT IT TO YOU!)

WHY?
BECAUSE IT DOESN'T BELONG TO YOU. ONLY THE PERSON IN THE PHOTO CAN DECIDE.

AND ONCE YOU PASS IT ON...
YOU CAN'T CONTROL WHERE IT GOES...

EVERYONE
UH-OH.
DING!
YOUR FRIEND

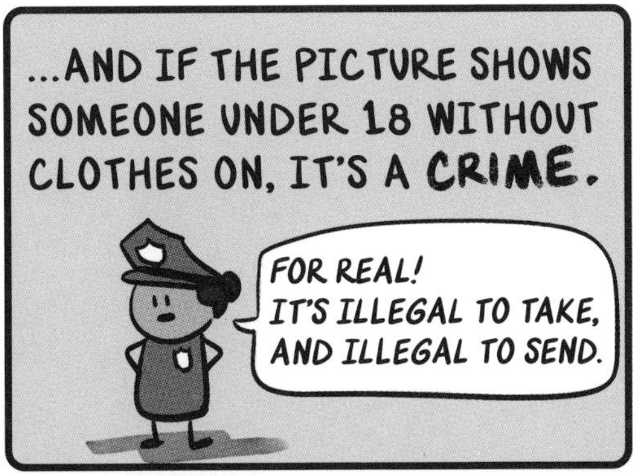
...AND IF THE PICTURE SHOWS SOMEONE UNDER 18 WITHOUT CLOTHES ON, IT'S A CRIME.
FOR REAL!
IT'S ILLEGAL TO TAKE, AND ILLEGAL TO SEND.

LEARNING TO RESPECT EACH OTHER IS HARD AT FIRST.

AAAH!

CONSENT
TAKES PRACTICE.

THE MORE THAT PEOPLE AROUND YOU PRACTICE CONSENT, THE MORE NATURAL IT IS FOR EVERYONE.

Woo!
Whee!

chapter 7 YOU TO THE RESCUE!

OK,

SO NOW YOU KNOW ABOUT SETTING YOUR OWN BOUNDARIES & LISTENING TO OTHERS.

BUT WHAT IF YOU NOTICE **SOMEONE ELSE** IN A BAD SITUATION?

UH-OH.
HEY! STOP!
YOU
OTHER FOLKS

4 WAYS TO HELP

(IF THE SITUATION DOESN'T FEEL SAFE, SKIP TO #4.)

1. BE DIRECT.
!
HELLO THERE! THAT'S NOT OK!
2. CHECK IN WITH THE PERSON IN TROUBLE.
AHEM
HOW'S IT GOING?
3. DISTRACT.
TACO TRUCK!
?
?
4. REPORT.
THEY NEED HELP.
trusted adult

YOU CAN'T KEEP EVERYONE **SAFE...**

AW...BUT I JUST PUT THIS CAPE ON!

BUT YOU **CAN** MAKE A DIFFERENCE WITH YOUR SUPPORT.

I BELIEVE YOU.
I'M HERE FOR YOU.
IT'S NOT YOUR FAULT.
THANKS.

SUPPORT YOUR FRIENDS.
I CARE ABOUT YOU.

OFFER TO ASSIST WHEN SOMEONE IS BEING MISTREATED.
HOW CAN I HELP?

★ AND MOST IMPORTANT, LET THEM KNOW—

IT'S NOT THEIR FAULT IF SOMEONE CROSSES A BOUNDARY WITHOUT THEIR CONSENT.

chapter 8 STAY STRONG TOGETHER

EVERY FAMILY HAS DIFFERENT IDEAS ABOUT HOW MUCH BODILY AUTONOMY KIDS SHOULD HAVE.

GO GET US DINNER!

15,000 YEARS AGO

SOME PEOPLE TRY TO RESPECT KIDS' AUTONOMY:

WHICH ONE WOULD YOU LIKE TO WEAR?
THAT ONE!

AND OTHERS FEEL LIKE THE ADULTS SHOULD DECIDE:

HERE'S YOUR OUTFIT.
UM, OK?
5 MINUTES LATER...
UHHH...

IT'S GREAT WHEN YOUR FAMILY **SUPPORTS** YOUR CHOICES: BUT IF THEY **DON'T**:

YOU HAVE A FEW OPTIONS:

REACH OUT TO SUPPORTIVE FRIENDS.
TALK TO THE ADULTS IN YOUR LIFE TO EXPLAIN HOW YOU FEEL.
THINK ABOUT WHAT YOU'LL DO DIFFERENTLY AS AN ADULT.

IF IT'S **MORE** THAN ANNOYING AND SOMEONE:

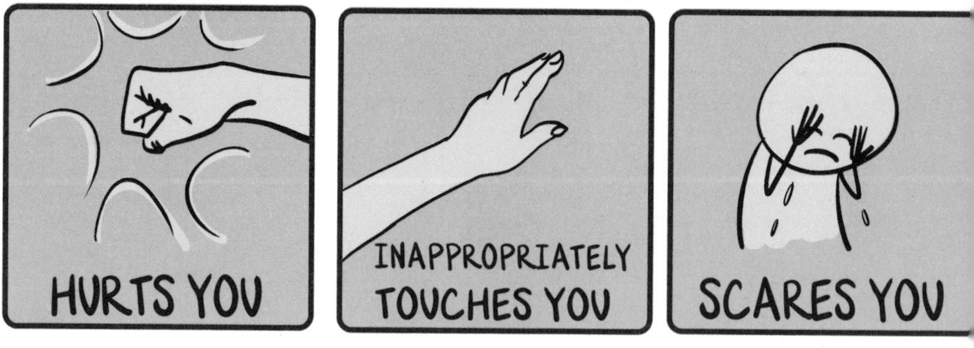
HURTS YOU
INAPPROPRIATELY TOUCHES YOU
SCARES YOU

OR IF YOU'RE CONFUSED,

REACH OUT FOR HELP. (Turn the page for resources.)

FIND YOUR CREW.

NOT EVERY PERSON IN OUR LIVES PRACTICES CONSENT.

THAT'S WHY IT'S SO IMPORTANT TO BUILD STRONG FRIENDSHIPS.

HAVING PEOPLE IN YOUR LIFE WHO SUPPORT YOU, LISTEN TO YOU & RESPECT YOU WILL HELP YOU THRIVE.

(& you'll do the same for them!)

HELP!

IF SOMEONE HAS CROSSED YOUR BOUNDARIES & YOU ARE SCARED, HURT, CONFUSED, OR FEEL UNSAFE- REACH OUT FOR HELP.

TRUSTED ADULT
LIKE A PARENT, TEACHER, OR COUNSELOR
EMERGENCY NUMBER LIKE 911
LOCAL SERVICES OR HOTLINE
1-800-4-A-CHILD
ONLINE HELP
CHILDHELP.ORG

BECAUSE THERE ARE SOME THINGS KIDS **CAN'T CONSENT** TO.

SO KNOW THAT IT'S **NOT** YOUR FAULT

& YOU'RE NOT ALONE!
ME TOO!

CONNECT WITH PEOPLE WHO CAN GIVE YOU SUPPORT & HELP YOU TO BE SAFE!

☆ ACKNOWLEDGMENTS ☆

To my editors, Lisa Yoskowitz and Laura Horsley—your smart, thoughtful comments and suggestions really helped this book gel. It's been such a pleasure to collaborate with you, and it shows in the strength of the final project.

To Karina Granda for her incredible art direction and helpful feedback on the technical aspects, and to Annie McDonnell, Laura Hambleton, and the whole team at Hachette who worked to make the book so beautiful.

Thanks to my agent, Molly Ker Hawn at the Bent Agency, for being my publishing "doula"; I'm so thankful to have your knowledge, guidance, and skills in my corner.

Special thanks to my expert readers for their quick and insightful feedback on the content: Kristy Kosak, Sarah Potts, Kim Alaburda, and Jess Burke.

For Sarah Brian, who is the perfect person to call for inspiration, collaboration, or commiseration.

For Barbara and Doug Brian, who still feed me breakfast some days.

For Laura Westberg, whose wise counsel helps me stay grounded and sane(ish) in times of both uncertainty and joy.

For Julie Talbutt, my rock.

RACHEL BRIAN

is the founder, owner, and principal animator of Blue Seat Studios. She is best known for her work on *Tea Consent* and *Consent for Kids*, short videos explaining consent that have been translated into over 20 languages and had more than 150 million views worldwide. A lifelong artist, Rachel is a former researcher and an educator, having taught physiology, biology, and math to high school and college students. She lives with her three children and an adorably ugly dog named Harvey in Providence, Rhode Island.